STAND & WITHSTAND INTEGRITY GROUP PRESENTS:
SUPPLY & DEMAND EDUCATION

THE DEMAND

EDUCATION REFORM WE NEED
INITIATED BY THE STUDENTS WE LEAD

DEMAND IT
WHAT "GO TO SCHOOL AND GET AN EDUCATION" REALLY MEANS
DANIEL C. MANLEY

DEMAND IT
WHAT "GO TO SCHOOL AND GET AN EDUCATION" REALLY MEANS
WORKBOOK
DANIEL C. MANLEY

RECORD IT
EDUCATIONAL REFLECTION JOURNAL
WHAT "HOW WAS SCHOOL TODAY" REALLY MEANS

Copyright © Daniel C. Manley 2022

Layout: Stand & Withstand Integrity Group LLC
Cover Design: Stand & Withstand Integrity Group LLC
Editor: Thelma Manley
Adapted By: Zoë Manley, Kenton Manley, Lemuel Manley, Azana Manley

All rights reserved. No part of this book may be reproduced or used in any manner without the prior written permission of the copyright owner, except for the use of brief quotations in a book review.

Publisher and author make no guarantees regarding the level of success you may experience by following the recommendations and principles contained in this book, and you accept the risk that results will differ for everyone. Examples presented are exemplar results, which may not be the outcome for all, and are not intended to represent or guarantee that you will achieve similar results.

To request permissions, contact the publisher:
CONTACT@standwithstand.org

Library of Congress Cataloging-in-Publication Data has been applied for.
ISBN 979-8-218-02557-1 (Hard Cover)

Printed in the United States of America
First Edition September 2022

Stand & Withstand Integrity Group LLC
P.O. Box 782771
Wichita, KS 67278
STANDWITHSTAND.ORG

CONTENTS

INTRODUCTION: I OWE YOU 2
   WHAT DO YOU OWE ME? 2

CHAPTER ONE: HELP THE HELPER 6
   HOW DO I GET AN EDUCATION? 6
   WHAT IS AN EDUCATION? 7
   WHY DO I GO TO SCHOOL? 8
   WHAT DOES IT MEAN TO BE CERTIFIED? 9
   WHAT DOES IT MEAN TO BE QUALIFIED? 10
   WHAT DO TEACHERS DO FOR MY EDUCATION? 12
   WHY DON'T TEACHERS EDUCATE? 13
   HOW DO TEACHERS BECOME EDUCATORS? 13
   WHY PICK TEACHING OVER EDUCATING? 15

CHAPTER TWO: BECOME A STUDENT 18
   HOW DOES A KID MAKE AN ADULT DO SOMETHING? 18
   HOW DOES A KID GET AN EDUCATION? 19
   WHAT IS A STUDENT? 20
   WHAT IS INTEGRITY? 21
   WHAT DOES INTEGRITY DO FOR MY EDUCATION? 22

CHAPTER THREE: BE A STUDENT 24
   HOW DOES A STUDENT ACT? 24
   HOW DOES A STUDENT ACT AT HOME? 25
   HOW DOES A STUDENT ACT AT SCHOOL? 27
   WHAT SHOULD A STUDENT DO BEFORE LEAVING SCHOOL? 28
   DOES STUDENT BEHAVIOR GUARANTEE AN EDUCATION? 30

CHAPTER FOUR: MAINTAIN THE STANDARD 32
   WHAT HAPPENS IF KIDS DON'T GET EDUCATED? 32
   WHAT HAPPENS IF STUDENT'S DON'T GET EDUCATED? 33

- HOW CAN I MAKE TEACHERS RESPONSIBLE FOR EDUCATING? 34
- WHAT IS SCHOOL LIKE FOR A STUDENT? 35
- WHAT'S THE EDUCATIONAL VALUE CONTINUUM™? 36
- HOW DO I KEEP MY TIME FROM BEING WASTED? 38
- DO TEACHERS LIE? 39
- IS SCHOOL ANY FUN? 40

CHAPTER FIVE: BE IN CONTROL 42
- WHAT POWER DO I HAVE TO CONTROL ANYTHING? 42
- WHAT IS AUTHORITY? 42
- WHAT AUTHORITY DO TEACHERS HAVE? 43
- WHAT AUTHORITY DO I HAVE TO USE MY POWER? 44
- WHAT HAPPENS WHEN I'M SELF-DISCIPLINED? 45

CHAPTER SIX: DON'T ACCEPT NO 48
- ARE TEACHERS HYPOCRITES? 48
- WHY BLAME TEACHERS IF THE SYSTEM IS BROKEN? 49
- HOW DO I MAKE A DEMAND? 50
- WHAT HAPPENS AFTER I MAKE A DEMAND? 52

CHAPTER SEVEN: CALL FOR BACKUP 54
- WHO ARE MY ALLIES? 54
- HOW DO I MAKE AN ALLIANCE STRONG? 55
- HOW WILL MY ALLIES BE THERE FOR ME? 56
- I NEVER ACCEPT NO? 58

CONCLUSION: YOU OWE YOURSELF 60
- WHAT DO I OWE MYSELF? 60

ABOUT THE AUTHOR 64

DEDICATION:

To every child being told to, "Go to school and get an education." Use this book to make that happen.

INTRODUCTION:
I OWE YOU

WHAT DO YOU OWE ME?

My child, I owe you my best effort in setting you up for a life of fulfillment. It was not your choice to be born. Your family, home, and quality of life are the result of other people's decisions. Now, as you are four years old and complaining about how long it's taking to turn five, I can't help but feel anxious about your future and how much control I have over it.

A good education is often considered the best way to put kids on a road to success and prepare them for the future. Unfortunately, the place society plans for you to get your education often struggles to get the job done. When you talk to people who attend school, work in schools, and make big decisions on how schools should run, you find out most of what schools should be doing is not being done well. Sometimes, and my experience and research make me comfortable telling you this, it's not being done at all. Because of this, I'm going to share information that all kids should have before they go to school expecting to get an education – pay attention.

In school, you are often considered a good student if you're focused on making your parents proud, following instructions, getting good grades, and graduating. Because the education system is so broken, however, it has even become difficult for "good students" to graduate with confidence that they're educated. Getting an education is hard to do because many of the people who work in our schools can't tell you what an education actually is (this is a major symptom of an educational disease I call the *Miseducation of Education*™).

Many of the adults who work to help young people get an education refer to themselves as educators. Yet, most of them have a difficult time being clear when trying to explain what education is. Just because someone is a teacher doesn't mean they're an educator. So, attending classes and completing the assigned tasks doesn't guarantee you an education. You are responsible for more than carrying a backpack, following instructions, doing homework, and getting good grades. Because getting an education is so important, turning five and starting school is really how you begin to take responsibility for your own life.

Living a fulfilled life, one where happiness and success are more constant than sadness and failure, is not as easy as most people want you to believe. All around the world, people live in homes, work jobs, and stay in relationships they are not fully satisfied with. I imagine most of them would live differently if they knew how. Education, as it has been studied, is one of the biggest reasons why people live the way they do. If you don't take advantage of this opportunity, your life is likely to be harder than it has to be. For this reason, allowing you to go to school without this information is neglectful, irresponsible, and it robs you of an opportunity to start your adult life on the right path. As a parent, I can't allow this to happen to you.

You will know the truth about what school and education are. You will know who you need to be and what you need to do to get an education. You will know what power and authority you have. You will know how to get help when things get too difficult. Knowing how to do these things will be very helpful as you work to get an education. Read this book and use my experience to learn lessons that would be difficult to learn on your own.

There is only one way to make sure your K-12 career gives you the kind of experience that will prepare you to be successful in life. Walk into every one of your classes, raise your hand, and claim your education like it's already yours. You must *Demand It*. Please, my dear child, let me educate you on exactly what that means.

Power concedes nothing without a demand.

Frederick Douglas

CHAPTER ONE:
HELP THE HELPER

HOW DO I GET AN EDUCATION?

Before you can get one, you must be clear on what an education actually is. When people say, "Go to school and get an education," they mean well. They know how important education is and want you to take school seriously. Most adults stress to kids how important it is to have an education, but they don't really explain what an education is.

Education is not an ordinary item that can be picked up as easily as chicken nuggets at a fast-food restaurant. All throughout the past, the strongest nations and most successful people have relied on education more than anything else to make progress. At this point in history, as far advanced as technology has become, not being educated is like losing your birthright. This is why being told to get an education happens as often as it does. Society has been consistent in preaching this message, but they have done it incompletely. Until you can say for sure that you know what an education is, getting one is going to be incredibly hard.

> **…not being educated is like losing your birthright.**

WHAT IS AN EDUCATION?

An education is a unique assortment of information that you possess, understand, know how to use, and benefit from. I say *unique assortment* because every life is different and needs a special mix of information to be lived. I say *possess* because you need to understand information well enough to say, "I got it!" You should be so confident that you've got it, that no one should need to reteach it to you. When I say *understand*, I mean you get an understanding of how the information has meaning in your life. This means that you know how to make the information you learn important in a personal way. If you don't know how to make information mean something to you personally, you won't have any reason to use it.

Until you *know how to use* information, you're trading education for basic learning. Being able to learn is an important step in the process, but education requires you to use what you learn. Learning about gravity will give you something interesting to talk about. When you get an education in gravity, you're careful not to fall or jump off objects at dangerous heights to prevent yourself from being hurt. The possibility of saving your life gives this information more value than storing it in your brain ever could. This is what makes information worth having in the first place – you can *benefit from* it.

Please don't hear me saying that you benefit in some fairytale, "Learning is fundamental," kind of way. Real education offers an, "Oh! That's what I get out of this," kind of reward. Things that could become real are so clear and possible in your mind that you accept them as true. Even if you haven't seen it before, the possibility is so real that it makes you believe.

Only when you *possess* (1), *understand* (2), *know how to use* (3), and *benefit from* (4) a unique assortment of information are you educated. Without all four of these parts, you can call yourself smart, knowledgeable, or well-informed. To say that you're educated, however, would only be correct if you're using this definition for education. This definition uncovers what people need to get out of school to be successful in life. Unfortunately, our education system doesn't use this definition and our schools aren't set up to make sure this is what students are getting. As a result, people often grow up unsure about what they want to do in life. They get confused and upset because they can't figure out why school took so much time but rewarded them with so little.

WHY DO I GO TO SCHOOL?

Getting an education is so important that society wants to make sure every person has an opportunity to get one before adulthood. School is supposed to be the place where you get it. Society doesn't know who the next great medical researcher, war hero, Hall-of-Fame quarterback, president, social media influencer, or Supreme Court judge will be. To give all kids an opportunity to discover what they might want to become, we send them to school. School is supposed to show you the different possibilities in life. This way, when you're old enough to decide what you want to do, you can work toward living that life confidently with a strong educational foundation.

School is supposed to be the place that gives students space and opportunity to get an education. People don't always agree on what kind of education students should get, but education has always been the purpose of school. Because our system has not clearly defined what education is, schools can focus on anything that helps turn kids into citizens that benefit society. The type of job, career, or future you want doesn't matter to most people if you add to society in a positive way. Schools are more focused on making you the type of citizen that benefits society than helping you get an education for your unique life. Because schools are so confident that they're doing a good thing, doing the right thing has become a challenge that's scary and uncomfortable.

The way schools work has changed throughout history, but what they want to accomplish hasn't. Older generations need younger generations to be educated for society to be productive and stable in the future. Educated people help their communities succeed, so future generations being uneducated is bad for society overall. Therefore, the K-12 school experience is societies way of helping you get certified with your most basic education.

WHAT DOES IT MEAN TO BE CERTIFIED?

To be certified is to have an official person or place that's trustworthy provide proof that you're "good enough" at something. This is usually done with a document that communicates, "Yes; this person is educated in what they're saying they have an education in." I'll give you an example.

To become a surgeon, an individual must prove they're educated to a lot of people in different places. If they can't, they won't be able to move forward in the process. Our medical system would be in serious trouble if college professors gave grades, universities gave degrees, medical schools gave certificates, medical licensors gave scores, residency programs gave reference letters, or hospitals gave jobs without proof that a surgeon had an education. They would be letting someone become a doctor, and do life-threatening surgeries, without proof that this person is good enough to do so successfully.

This is how most professions work. Teachers don't become principals, cadets don't become Sergeants, and mechanics don't become master technicians without multiple people agreeing that they're good enough and allowing them to be certified. More important than being certified, however, is your ability to show others that you're qualified.

WHAT DOES IT MEAN TO BE QUALIFIED?

Being qualified means using your knowledge and skills to prove you're "good enough" to do a certain job or task successfully. There's not a certified chef preparing the meals at every restaurant you eat at. The athletes you cheer for don't need to have a certificate to prove they can play their sports. The entertainers and actors that sing songs and star in the movies you love aren't required to have a certificate before they perform. When people can just show you how good they are, they're putting their education on display. They are proving they're qualified.

The world is too big for everyone's abilities to be seen by every person who needs to know they have them. Society uses institutions and systems to classify people as certified. We trust certain places to tell us who has proven they're good enough because we believe these places are trustworthy. Almost every profession and serious business will ask you to be certified for what you say you're qualified to do. And for this, there will always be some version of school.

I say some version of school because school's not just a building with classrooms. Any place that gives you space and opportunity to get an education can be a school. The playground is school for an athlete. Spending countless hours imagining a make-believe fantasy world is a normal school day for an author. A teenager's messy bedroom could be the school where a professional gamer trains on a PC, PlayStation, or Xbox. Going to a place or doing an activity with a student mindset can transform any place into a school.

Kids go to school with one of five different mindsets. The *child* is not concerned with learning or education. Their basic needs, feelings, and comfort are what they focus on. Asking them to do other things will probably upset them; their time at school is like daycare. The *pupil* participates in school activities, but staying out of trouble and people-pleasing are the main reasons why. To them, school is like working a job just to get paid or keep the boss quiet. The *student* knows what an education is and uses their time at school to get one. The *active participant* is a focused student who wants the most out of life rather than just an education in general. The e*ngaged agent* is a serious student who wants the best education to achieve specific life goals. You'll need to be at least a student to get an education.

> ...school's not just a building with classrooms.

K-12 schools are supposed to produce mature young adults

who are ready to benefit society. Sadly, it has become easy to be certified by this education system without proving you're qualified. Companies are saying, "These graduates aren't good enough." Colleges are saying, "These high schoolers aren't good enough." High schools are saying, "These middle schoolers aren't good enough." Middle schools are saying, "These elementary kids aren't good enough." Elementary schools are saying, "These parents aren't doing enough." Parents are saying, "These teachers aren't doing enough." The system society trusts to make sure kids are being educated is no longer trustworthy. Be sure that you're qualified for higher levels by making sure teachers are doing what they're supposed to do for your education.

WHAT DO TEACHERS DO FOR MY EDUCATION?

Teachers use lessons and activities to inform others who know less than they do. Educators teach lessons that are designed to help students get an education. You need to see how teachers and educators are different because most people use these two words like they mean the same thing. Being a teacher is not what makes someone an educator. Teachers give information and check to see how well it's understood. An educator teaches, then help student's see how they can use and benefit from the information in a general or personal way.

Teachers do the first half of an educator's job. The information they teach is the foundation for every education. It's impossible to get an education without a teacher. For that reason, this profession should be given a lot of respect. Teachers start the process for every job and career that society needs to be filled. However, it takes more than teaching for education to be the result. If humanity is going to do more than just work for survival, our teachers must do more than teach. They must educate.

WHY DON'T TEACHERS EDUCATE?

Teachers are certified to teach their subject, manage classrooms, and check for how much kids learn. Education is talked about as the goal, but it's never clearly defined or outlined as the daily target of instruction. If someone can't tell you what an education is, then that person can't honestly say education is what they're focused on or helping you work toward. This is the *Miseducation of Education*™. Basically, the system preparing teachers to help students get an education doesn't make them prove they're qualified as educators before they get certified.

When I went to college to become a teacher, I didn't get educated on being an educator. I got an education in teaching. I was never taught how to take information and teach others how to use it or benefit from it in their real lives. I wasn't told that this was my job, nor was it explained that this was the true focus of my daily work. Teachers don't educate because educating is not what the system has taught, trained, or required them to do. If teachers are going to be expected to educate, they must first become educators.

HOW DO TEACHERS BECOME EDUCATORS?

Teachers become educators when they make education the direct goal of their teaching. Education is the ingredient that makes school what it's meant to be. The uses and benefits of learned information are what boost learning up to education. If the uses and benefits of learned information are left out of daily instruction, the main ingredients of education are being left out of school. Far too often, as crazy as it sounds, education is being left out of the educational experience.

Is buttery popcorn enough to get you into a movie-theatre, or do you actually want to see a film on the screen? Are you going to wait in that long Chick-Fil-A line if they don't have chicken? Getting a strawberry-lemonade, some waffle fries, and a "my pleasure" response doesn't make the trip worth it. How interested would you be in going to Disney World if the environment, rides, or experience were missing the Disney theme? Such bad customer service is normal in the education system. Because of it, teachers are too busy trying to keep unsatisfied customers happy to focus on an educator's job. Society complains about the school experience, but this incomplete version of education is the product being offered by the system most regularly.

When teachers are focused on teaching, attending school as a child or pupil becomes normal for kids. Not attending school as a student allows the quality of your education to go down. Being asked to do activities that are missing the main ingredient will make you ask, "Why do I have to do this," or "Why do I have to come here?" Asking these types of questions is a clear sign that education is missing from your school experience. The longer you experience school without the main ingredient, the harder it becomes for you to be a student. If teachers don't hear students asking these questions, they won't see a problem with the work they're doing.

A teacher's job is teaching, but the system says their goal is for you to get an education. Without educating, not even the hardest working teachers can accomplish the system's goal. The job teachers are responsible for doing is being done most of the time. For teachers to become educators, however, they have to remain unbroken within a broken system. When you're a student, you help them to do so. Faced with an option to teach or educate, educating must be their choice.

WHY PICK TEACHING OVER EDUCATING?

Until now, the choice between teaching and educating was not really a choice. When everything about the system says teach, supports teaching, and encourages teachers, what else is there to do? Because the education system is not set up to make education the focus of daily operations, anyone in the system who picks educating over teaching is seen as different. Also, when there are major issues in society that need fixing, work that has nothing to do with what teachers are supposed to teach gets pushed into schools.

Schools allow health professionals to come in and help kids be healthier. Meetings with therapists and mindfulness groups take students out of class to help with their feelings. Social workers, college advisors, behavior specialist, motivational speakers, and other support groups all have a place in schools. While these things can be helpful in their own way, they also make it harder for teachers to pick educating over teaching. Teaching is a hard thing to do all by itself. Being asked to juggle extra tasks at the same time just makes things unfair. On top of that, we ask them to be the parents, coaches, volunteers, and supporters that kids don't have. All these extras take away from their families, hobbies, and planning time. Most of these things earn them no extra money. Simply stated, it's a lot.

It would be wrong to say teachers don't educate because they're lazy or only care about earning a paycheck. It would be irresponsible, and it's simply not true. Some teachers are bad. Every profession has people that don't do their job well. However, when teachers aren't busy doing the extra work society asks them to do, they're doing their jobs. They are teaching. Everything about how they were certified and what they're job focuses on is about teaching. If teachers are going to make education the focus of their job, become educators, they must work against a system that makes school a very difficult place to get educated.

Despite all of this, you are still expected to get an education. It's hard work, but it is possible. It's possible because every educator must first be a teacher. Many teachers never become educators because few kids attend school as students. Caring for children and teaching pupils does not require the main ingredient. Without uses and benefits, learning does not become education. Without education, that building does not become a school. You need to become a student to help teachers see that the system's main ingredient is missing. Require them to be educators so they'll supply you with what you need. Without your help, the system may stay broken forever.

> **Many teachers never become educators because few kids attend school as students.**

CHAPTER TWO:
BECOME A STUDENT

HOW DOES A KID MAKE AN ADULT DO SOMETHING?
The only way a kid can make an adult do something is by reminding them of the beliefs that are important to them. This is tricky because most adults call it disrespectful for a kid to give them instructions or tell them what to do. Don't tell them what to do, just give them polite reminders. The best way to make teachers become educators, when the system won't even do it, is by reminding them that education is the goal. By making yourself a certain type of learner, education becomes the focus it needs to be for teachers to become educators. It shouldn't be your job to correct their focus, but this is how broken the system is.

Adults don't expect you to be a source of wisdom because you know so little about how the world works. If they haven't helped you make sense of something, adults are quite surprised when you know what you're talking about. Being a kid doesn't prevent you from being intelligent, responsible, or capable. Being a kid means there's a lot you don't know, haven't seen or done, and get curious about. This makes you a threat to yourself and others because it can be easy to make dangerous mistakes.

Childhood isn't about being powerless and controlled, it's about getting an education in life. When you get an education and mature, people trust you to be responsible and control your own life. Because of how badly you could hurt yourself or someone else by making a dangerous mistake, adults focus more on protecting you than preparing you for independence. If you're not ready for adulthood when

> **Making the wrong mistake, or having a bad enough injury before turning 18, could ruin your life altogether.**

you turn 18, we can always help you for a few more years. Making the wrong mistake, or having a bad enough injury before turning 18, could ruin your life altogether. Raising kids and growing up, like I said, it's tricky. Because kids aren't often raised to think for themselves, getting an education when you're still a kid can be difficult.

HOW DOES A KID GET AN EDUCATION?

If you're going to get an education as a kid, you have to make it clear that you're a serious student. Think about it. Does walking into a restaurant stop you from being hungry? Is your stomach filled when you look at the menu, order a meal, or have food brought to the table? Even if you were at your favorite restaurant, you still wouldn't be satisfied. Until you've eaten everything on the plate, you haven't got what you went to the restaurant to get.

The getting of an education takes much more than just sitting at a table and ordering from a menu. A school can't give you an education. Teachers can't give you an education. Your parents can't give you an education. An educator can't give you an education. None of the people working at a restaurant can fill your empty belly. If you don't pick up a fork and clear your plate, you're going to stay hungry. Similarly, no combination of people or events can give you an education. You have to get it yourself. The only thing other people can do, even at their very best, is give you an opportunity to get one.

This is why most kids don't know if they have an education. Even if they finish school with good grades and go to college, most can't tell you what an education is or say for sure if they got one in school. You get an education by refusing to wait on other people to give you one as a child or a pupil. It can't happen that way. You have to be a student and go get it.

WHAT IS A STUDENT?

A student is an individual who is active and involved in getting an education. They attend school and approach learning with genuine interest and curiosity. Most importantly, a student knows what an education is. Without knowing what an education is, you can't say you're putting action towards getting one. No matter how active or involved you are in school, the best you can be without trying to get all four parts of an education is a hardworking pupil.

> **No one can be more responsible for getting an education than the student.**

Being a student when you're still a kid is hard work because kids are used to other people being responsible for the important things in their lives. No one can be more responsible for getting an education than the student. Just because someone puts you in a place where you can get all four parts of an education, it doesn't mean you've actually gotten them. Because the system is broken, and education is not set up to be the focus, finishing school doesn't equal getting an education. How you attend K-12 schools determines what they prepare you to do. If you're a child, making school a daycare, it prepares you to depend on others to take care of you. If you're a pupil, making school an institution, it prepares you to work for small prizes and be obedient to a system. When you're a student, allowing school to be what it's meant to be, it really can prepare you for a life of fulfillment.

A student knows the difference between teachers and educators, learning and education, and can tell which parts of an education are being left out of a lesson. If a student feels they're being offered an educational opportunity that's not good enough, they have the right to demand better. To be clear, to *demand* is to ask for something with confidence and refuse to be told no. Every school believes it's important to help kids get an education. This belief makes "No" an unacceptable answer when you're asking for a better educational opportunity. The brokenness of the system makes things hard for teachers, but that's not your fault. You know what an education is, and you know it's value. This is what you need to believe, and this is who you need to be for teachers to accept that they must be educators. Having student integrity will go a long way to help you do so.

<u>WHAT IS INTEGRITY?</u>

Integrity is a constant display of thoughts, words, and actions that show the same thing. Thoughts are the starting place for everything humans do. Although, if thoughts never cause words to be spoken or actions to be shown, what do they really do? The way you think about things is the way you should speak about them. When you speak about things a certain way, you should have behaviors that match. Your words and actions are evidence of what you think. A consistent balance of these separate parts is integrity.

People often use words like honest, good, or moral when they define integrity. Schools like to say, "Integrity is doing what's right when no one is looking." They say these things because most people want to live a good life and do good things. This is why having integrity usually leads to what's honest, good, or moral. Seeing people do bad things, when they say they want a good life, makes it hard to know what they believe. Having integrity means standing by your beliefs so they're always clear. To have a lack of integrity is hypocrisy.

This is important because having integrity means being consistent. Don't say, "I don't like school," unless you're taking on that belief and you're ready to have those behaviors. Some kids get good grades but talk about hating school all the time. Who are they trying to be? Do they want to be uneducated, or are they just mad about the parts of school that feel like daycare and meaningless work? Most kids say, "I want to be happy, successful, and have a good life." Is that what you want? Well, you need an education for those things. It's hard to take you seriously as a student if integrity doesn't show you value education.

WHAT DOES INTEGRITY DO FOR MY EDUCATION?

Education gives you the best chance to live the kind of life you want, but we have an education system that lacks integrity. This is because they've never used a specific definition for education, had a clear process for helping kids get one, or figured out a way to guarantee the job gets done. This is why student integrity shines such a bright light on the system's hypocrisy. To let that light shine as brightly as it can, embrace these beliefs and let them be the start of your integrity as a student:

STUDENT INTEGRITY THOUGHTS

1) I need to possess, understand, know how to use, and benefit from information to be educated.
2) I need to focus on education to make the best use of my time.
3) I need to control myself well enough for other people to trust me.
4) I need to be more responsible for my education than anyone else.
5) I need to earn my education; it can't be given to me.

After you accept these thoughts as your own, getting your words and actions to line up with them is the next step. If you don't have integrity, people won't know what to believe about you. This takes the pressure off them to be educators and give you a real school experience. When you start saying you want a real education, there will also be pressure on you. People will expect you to be the student you say you are. Embracing these ideas is your first step to becoming a student, but you'll need more than thoughts and beliefs to really be one. You'll need action.

> **When you start saying you want a real education, there will also be pressure on you.**

CHAPTER THREE:
BE A STUDENT

HOW DOES A STUDENT ACT?

A student has behaviors that are consistently focused on getting an education. Their behaviors are proof they want to be in school and plan on getting something out of the experience. Students will do the hard work it takes to get an education. They aren't happy to just have good days and stay out of trouble. They want to know they're making progress. You haven't done enough to call yourself a student by walking into a school or classroom. There is so much more that goes into it than that.

Do you know what makes you a customer? A person can spend hours in a mall looking at, testing out, trying on, and asking about products and still not be a customer. The only thing that makes you a customer is buying what a business is selling. Until you trade your money for their product or service, you're only a *potential customer*. If nothing's being bought, the work and effort of employees is to convince potential customers to buy something. In school, education is the product. Helping students get an education is the service schools are supposed to provide. For you to be a student, an *education customer*, you have to pay the price for the product a school offers. That price is hard work, not blind obedience.

No one in history has had lasting happiness, wealth, or success without first becoming a student and getting an education in something. It has never happened before, and it never will. Challenge this idea if you want to, but you'll struggle to find fulfillment until you accept that it's true. Behaviors that prove you're a student show people your beliefs and help you to get an education. I'm not just talking about at school. If you're going to be a student, you need to get your behaviors right at home.

> **Preparing kids to go to school with education as their focus doesn't really happen.**

HOW DOES A STUDENT ACT AT HOME?

At home, the actions of a student help them prepare to get an education at school. Being *prepared* means doing things that must be done before you can do what you want to do. Preparing kids to go to school with education as their focus doesn't really happen. School is often painted as a fun place with cool activities and interesting people. As work gets harder and starts feeling pointless, kids will focus more on spending time away from school than preparing to be a student in the classroom. Working hard, just to say you had a good day and didn't get in trouble, isn't a reward for most kids after 3rd grade. If you're not prepared to be a student by then, it's hard to see school as a place that helps you prepare for adulthood.

Having the right actions before you go to school stems from the thoughts at the end of the last chapter. To show you are prepared to go to school as a student, check your actions and make sure they match those beliefs. Whether it's the night before school or in the morning when you wake up, there are lots of decisions for you to make so your behaviors match the *Student Integrity Thoughts*.

What time you go to bed at night or wake up in the morning may be different from kids who aren't preparing to get an education. Students can't afford to fall asleep in class and miss something. What you plan to eat for breakfast, lunch, or a snack could affect how much energy you have or how healthy you are. Students know how important it is to have the right energy for a long day of education seeking. What you focus on while back-to-school shopping may be different from a child or pupil. A student has to focus on buying things that make education easier to get. Looking for attention, compliments, and friends makes it difficult to get clothes and school supplies that are best for a student.

Having expensive clothes and electronics, eating the tasty snacks or lunch items others always want, or being able to brag about how late you stayed up watching Netflix might make you one of the "cool kids". I'd love to tell you those things mean nothing, but that's not true. Also, there's no rule against being both cool and a student. What's most important, however, is how you decide to invest your energy. Spending more time, money, and focus on being cool than being a student is a poor decision. Whatever "cool" you earn in school means nothing in the adult world, but the education you get from being a student can last a lifetime.

This kind of focus and seriousness has to happen if you're going to be prepared to be a student at school. Questioning your actions to make sure they're student-like prevents you from entering school as a child or pupil. What you eat, what you wear, what you take to school in your backpack, where you sit on the bus, who you call your friends, and plenty of other choices have actions that will make you more of a student than others. It takes work, but it gets easier the more you convince yourself that being a student and getting an education is worth it. Trust me, my child; it's worth it. The more prepared you are to be a student when you're at home, the easier it'll be for you when you get to school.

HOW DOES A STUDENT ACT AT SCHOOL?

The actions of a student allow a school's time and resources to be used for education. A student in a school should be like a kid in a candy store. You've seen the movie. Anyone who visits Willie Wonka's chocolate factory and leaves unhappy didn't do what they were supposed to do. If candy is what you want, there's no better place for you. If education is what you're looking for, school is the place to be. Because education is what society wants you to have, the law says you have to go to school. Jail is the only other place in the world that someone might be forced to go for as long as they have to go to school. It's pretty sad when I think about how often I've seen kids in school look and sound like prisoners. Everything about them says, "I just want to get out!"

> **A student in a school should be like a kid in a candy store.**

Most kids focus so much on getting out of school that they don't use the space and opportunity to prepare for the life they want afterwards. Think about running away from a wild animal.

Be A Student

If getting away from that beast is the only thing you're thinking about, how do you keep yourself on track to get where you really want to go? It's easy to get lost and confused if what's behind you is getting more attention than what you have in front of you. A student uses school to get an education and plan for the future. Student behaviors, especially at school, help to do just that.

The way you look and sound at school tells people what you're there for. If you're in the right place on time, have your supplies organized and ready, and help teachers keep education as the main focus of classroom activities, you're being a student. If you avoid gossiping and complaining, ask questions when you're curious or confused, and make comments that help you get an education, then you're being a student. Having actions opposite of these could mean you're going to school as a child or pupil. Not being a student makes it hard for you to do what needs to be done before you leave school.

WHAT SHOULD A STUDENT DO BEFORE LEAVING SCHOOL?

The most important behavior a student can have before leaving school (for the day, weekend, holiday break, summer vacation, or forever), is making sure they got what they went to school to get. *Success* is not as difficult as people make it seem; it's accomplishing specific goals. When you accomplish, achieve, or attain a goal, you're succeeding. If you succeed often enough in life, you'll be considered a success. When you leave school without getting an education, you make yourself unsuccessful as a student. Many high school seniors find themselves in this position at the end of every graduation season. Don't let it happen to you.

Asking yourself two questions at the end of every school day will make it clear whether you got an education or not. "How was school today," and "What did you learn today," aren't just questions parents ask to make small talk. They are checking to make sure the business that was supposed to take place in school actually did. Without all four parts of an education, remember, you can't call yourself educated. Answering these questions honestly and completely everyday makes it almost impossible for you to miss out on education.

Have you ever got home from a fast-food restaurant and found out that something was wrong with your order? People get mad enough to fight when the nugget count is wrong, extra sauce gets left out, or the "no onions" instruction gets ignored. How does a kid go to school for thirteen years and not know what an education is or if they're really getting one? Our education system has not made education the main item on the menu. Because of that, customers haven't been able to see how bad service actually is. Let me make it clear for you. Education is the only reason a school has for being in business. Also, the four ingredients for education are always the same. When a restaurant messes up your order, are you wrong to go back with your receipt and let them know so you can get what's rightfully yours? If you don't possess, understand, know how to use, and benefit from the information you're being taught, you should see it as a problem that needs to be fixed.

Do assignment instructions make education the clear focus

of your work? When a teacher goes through a lesson, do they point out all four parts of an education? If you complete a unit test, project, or presentation, can you see a complete education or not? If so, you are finding success and getting your education. If not, you need to ask questions and figure out why the most important item on the menu is being left out of your bag. This is how a student would act. Whether at home, during school, or before you leave, you should be acting like a student. By doing so, you're making your best effort to get an education.

DOES STUDENT BEHAVIOR GUARANTEE AN EDUCATION?

Having student behavior doesn't guarantee you get an education, but it makes it easier for you to demand one. Not acting like a student gives a broken system an excuse for you not getting an education. They can explain why a kid who has lots of behavior issues, missing assignments, or absences is struggling to get an education. To be a student and not get an education, however, means someone in the system has messed up. It'll be hard to blame you or deny your complaints if you have these behaviors:

STUDENT INTEGRITY BEHAVIORS

1) I have behaviors that match the *Student Integrity Thoughts*.
2) I get ready for school by preparing myself to be a student.
3) I look and sound like a student when I'm at school.
4) I work hard for educational growth, not to be obedient.
5) I look for *Educational Value* in all school activities.

Graduating should mean you're educated and prepared for

a higher level. It should make you a certified learner (a graduate). Being able to move up levels without proving you're educated is a flaw in the system that makes graduation meaningless. The celebration and diploma aren't proof of an education like they should be. Without getting an education, you haven't done what a student is supposed to do. Time is too important to waste; you'll be 18 years old before you know it. The system being broken is not your fault, but you're the only one who gets punished if you don't get an education.

> **The celebration and diploma aren't proof of an education like they should be.**

CHAPTER FOUR:
MAINTAIN THE STANDARD

WHAT HAPPENS IF KIDS DON'T GET EDUCATED?

If the system doesn't educate you, you'll be held responsible for how you live your adult life. It's not fair, I know, but the only real consequence for the system failing to educate kids is the bad reputation it gets. Other than that, blame gets passed between parents and teachers, and you'll be left to figure out adulthood without an education. When parents don't educate their kids on how to get an education, they're sending a child or pupil to school in a broken system. When classrooms are filled with kids who aren't students, teachers just do the job they were trained to do; they teach. If parents don't have to be qualified to educate before having kids, and teachers don't have to be qualified to educate before they can teach, it's hard to say whose fault it is when kids are uneducated.

Because the system hasn't made education the focus of schools, adults don't have to be qualified as parents, and teachers don't have to be qualified as educators, most kids go through school with the mindset of a child or pupil. When it's possible to finish a K-12 program "successfully" while being blindly obedient, uncaring, or lazy, most kids don't see a reason to do anything more? This is why having student integrity is so important. If students aren't being educated the problem is much easier to see.

WHAT HAPPENS IF STUDENTS DON'T GET EDUCATED?

If the system doesn't educate a student, they are asking for trouble. It's like them saying, "Education isn't what we do here. Just finish the work we gave you to do and get out!" Because students go to school looking and working for an education, not getting one means the school and/or teachers are stopping it from happening. Teachers are the only people in a student's life who must focus on education. Remember, teaching is the first half of an educator's job. Even if a teacher never becomes an educator, they still have more of a focus on education than anyone else. We can't say how qualified a parent, pastor, coach, or whoever else is to educate. However, a certified teacher is almost always certain to be in the classroom when students are present.

Talking about whose fault something is makes people feel better when they can say it's not theirs, but that doesn't resolve issues. Finding someone to blame and finding someone to take responsibility are not the same thing. Society is truly at fault for the brokenness of the education system. Waiting on society to fix all the problems that need to be fixed before our education system can work correctly, however, would take too long and cost too many kids a chance at getting an education. Making teachers responsible for helping students get an education is a much simpler task than asking them to accept blame for how broken the education system is.

HOW CAN I MAKE TEACHERS RESPONSIBLE FOR EDUCATING?

By making education the focus of everything you do, you make it something that teachers can only ignore on purpose. As an idea, the responsibility of educating students has already been accepted by teachers. Like I said before, the teaching profession doesn't really train, evaluate, or require teachers to educate. Their focus is teaching. So, until the system is fixed, a teacher who does the work of an educator is volunteering to do a more demanding job. How busy the profession keeps teachers makes it hard for them to focus on education, especially when they don't have students who are committed to it. You have to prevent this from happening.

Understand what an education is and how important it is for your future. Make sure you have the integrity of a student, so they can't treat you like you're just a child or pupil. Remember what school is for, so you don't get distracted by things that look like more fun. Doing these things prepare you to get your education. They also help teachers keep education as their focus and accept responsibility for cleaning up a broken system's mess.

As often as you can, let teachers know you're looking for an education. Meet-the-Teacher night or Open House could be the perfect time to introduce yourself as a student. With a few questions, and some insightful information, you can make it clear to your teachers that they will have to do more than what they were trained for. Make it their responsibility to educate you. Teachers may be surprised

> **As often as you can, let teachers know you're looking for an education.**

by these questions, but don't let that stop you. Asking these questions will tell you whether your instructor is prepared to be a teacher or an educator:

INSTRUCTOR ASSESSMENT QUESTIONS

1) Will your lessons include all four parts of an education?
2) Will your grades be proof that an education was earned?
3) Will your classroom management support me as a child, pupil, or student?

If you're asking these questions, you should be able to explain what they mean to teachers who need clarity. This will let them know how important getting an education is to you. These questions send a message and make you look like a student instead of a child or pupil. Introducing yourself like this is a great way to start, but being this person every day is what makes school a different place.

WHAT IS SCHOOL LIKE FOR A STUDENT?

School for a student is like a training facility for an athlete. Whatever you want to be, school gives you a chance to work on becoming that in the future. Imagine a baby bird being given a chance to fly for the first time. Living safely in a nest away from most of the world has put major limits on life. Because it makes flying possible, the edge of a nest offers a life-changing opportunity.

School, for a student, is like the jumping off point for that bird. It's an opportunity to start preparing for the adult life you want. The uses and benefits of learned information help you to control your life. Understand, the baby bird that isn't ready to fly should stay in the nest. This is not a game my child. Getting an education is the biggest responsibility you have as a kid. Take it seriously now because life won't give you another chance to make getting an education your only focus. You need to see how the things you learn and experience in school are useful and beneficial. To do it, you'll need the Educational Value Continuum™ (EVC).

WHAT'S THE EDUCATIONAL VALUE CONTINUUM™?

The Educational Value Continuum™ is a scale that shows you how learning can be useful and beneficial. On one end, *Minimum Functionality* tells you the most basic uses and benefits that an experience might be offering. *Maximum Possibility*, on the other end of the scale, tells you the highest possible uses and benefits that an experience can offer. When you're at school, it's your job to learn and figure out the educational value of what you're learning. This scale shows what options a daily school experience might bring. Finding an EVC item that helps you at school or in a specific class is not good enough. Use this scale to find EVC items that are useful and beneficial in your life outside of school. Work to see how a lesson can offer you:

MINIMUM FUNCTIONALITY

Learning this lesson has basic uses and benefits that help me in life:

1) **Ability** – I know how to do something.
2) **Skill** – I get better at doing something.
3) **Vocation** – I understand how to do a certain job.
4) **Relationship** – I interact and connect better with people.
5) **Mentality** – I form my own ideas about life.
6) **Mental Exercise** – I help my brain function better.

7) **Muscle Memory** – I help my body function better.
8) **Practice** – I work to improve an ability.
9) **Training** – I work intentionally to be excellent at a skill.
10) **Experience** – I become more aware, familiar, or educated.

MAXIMUM POSSIBILITY

Learning this lesson helps me make useful and beneficial discoveries about myself:

1) **Motivation** – I want to do something.
2) **Inspiration** – I have a strong internal motivation to achieve something.
3) **Higher Education** – I want an education past K-12.
4) **Career** – I want to get serious about a certain job/profession.
5) **Dream** – I want to accomplish a big goal.
6) **Invention** – I want to create something new.
7) **Innovation** – I want to improve something already created.
8) **Non-Profit** – I want to live my life in a way that helps me serve people.
9) **Fortune-500** – I want to live my life in a way that helps me gain financial wealth.
10) **Superhero** – I want to fulfill a purpose that helps me improve the world.

Finding the educational value of an experience adds a small nugget to a specific section of your overall education. The more nuggets you add to an EVC category, the more educated you become in that area. Learning without discovering the *Minimum Functionality* or *Maximum Possibility* of a lesson earns you half of an education at best. If teachers aren't helping you discover what a lesson adds to an EVC category, you're not getting the *Education Nugget* out of that experience and time is being wasted.

HOW DO I KEEP MY TIME FROM BEING WASTED?

Your time cannot be wasted unless it's spent on lessons, assignments, and activities that aren't fully educational. If you can't see all four parts of an education, you should ask for help or clarity. Until a teacher helps you possess, understand, know how to use, and benefit from the information they're teaching, they have not made education the focus of class. Get comfortable asking, "What's the educational value of this lesson?" If teachers hear this question often enough, they won't be able to waste time comfortably.

> **Get comfortable asking, "What's the educational value of this lesson?"**

Lessons that are supported by the EVC are a good use of time because they have clear value. You can break lessons down into sections by remembering this phrase, "*Expose* me to it, let me *explore* it, once I *experience* it, I *engage* in what *excites* me." Doing this during a lesson helps you track all five parts of the educational process and see what you're getting a chance to do:

1) **Exposure** – to see the educational value
2) **Exploration** – to learn and ask questions for clarity
3) **Experience** – to develop personal understanding and practical skills
4) **Engagement** – to work eagerly with defined goals
5) **Excitement** – to show genuine interest in new discoveries and possibilities

Without knowing the educational value of a lesson, you can't be sure how good you are or how well you're doing as a student. Because they don't follow a specific educational process, most teachers will teach content, assign practice work, reteach content, test your level of understanding, and restart the process with new content. You need an education to be prepared for adulthood, but the system only gives you proof that some level of learning took place. Education hasn't been made the focus of the system, so most of the grades you earn in school aren't proof of an education. If a lesson skips a step in the educational process, or educational value is missing, your time is being wasted. This also makes it hard to believe what teachers say about the progress you're making or how qualified you are for higher levels.

DO TEACHERS LIE?

It's hard to say, "Teachers lie," because I don't believe being dishonest is their goal. However, the system is so broken that it's hard to be honest when talking about results. Our schools have a lot of "graduates" that aren't confident, educated, or prepared for the future. This makes schools want to highlight things that are going well and tell a blurry truth. Real numbers are hard to look at and tough questions are hard to answer, so people would rather give teachers credit for how hard they're trying. To speak honestly about our broken system requires *education* to be a real thing. When a different definition than the one I gave you is used, education sounds

> ...schools want to highlight things that are going well and tell a blurry truth.

as strange as some mythical energy force.

Because no one can really tell you what education is, or how close you are to getting one, measuring the effort you put into it is what the system does. If you work hard and do what teachers ask you to do in class, you can get good grades easily and often. Trying hard to accomplish what schools ask you to do earns good grades, but those grades are measuring something different than the quality of your education (*Institutionalized Academic Obedience*). Don't trust what this broken system says about how good or prepared you are unless they give you real evidence. Until you can trust you're as good as their evidence says, ask these questions and track your own progress:

PERSONAL PROGRESS TRACKING
1) Does this assignment focus on a complete education?
2) Does this grade prove that I've been educated or just obedient?
3) Does this grade make the amount and/or quality of education I earned clear?

IS SCHOOL ANY FUN?

Absolutely! Please don't let how serious I sound about this make you think having fun at school is a problem. However, you need to understand that enjoying an experience is what fun truly is. The noise, laughter, and randomness that kids often call "fun" are just proof they're enjoying what they're doing. Quietly reading a book can be fun. Cleaning out a closet to take old clothes and toys to a donation center can be fun. Helping Gran in the kitchen while she bakes a cake, you know that's fun! Loud volume, high-energy, and foolishness aren't needed for fun. You should know this because many of America's schools are failing innocent kids. They do this by focusing on goals that are easier to see and more exciting than education.

Millions of young people go to school every day and have fun while failing to get an education. They fail by being taught and not educated. They fail because the blurry truth of *Institutionalized Academic Obedience* makes it hard to see just how broken the system is. If you plan to be educated and prepared for adulthood when you graduate, you must take control of your K-12 schooling. Being able to live a life of fulfillment is more fun than you can imagine. Raise your hand, ask tough questions, and use your power to set yourself up for that future.

CHAPTER FIVE:
BE IN CONTROL

WHAT POWER DO I HAVE TO CONTROL ANYTHING?

Power is the ability to do. If you have the ability to do something, it means that you have power. Honestly, the abilities you need to do most things in the adult world are abilities you'll have at a young age. You have the ability to do what any other capable person in the world can do in most cases. You have that power. What you don't have is enough education to do them correctly without issues. Because kids have a limited education, know so little about life, and have a hard time controlling themselves when they get excited, adults keep kids from using power to keep them from hurting themselves or others. Until you prove you know how to do things correctly without issues, adults will control how much power you use. It may feel like you don't have any power, but authority is really what you lack.

WHAT IS AUTHORITY?

To have authority, to be authorized, is to be given permission to use the power you have. Think about a game of Red-Light, Green-Light. If you can move from start line to finish line, you have power. It doesn't matter if you're crawling, hopping, sprinting, in a wheelchair, or walking on your hands; the power is there. What matters is that you limit yourself and only do what you've been given direct permission to do. Doing anything more than what you are given permission to do is asking for trouble. It's really that simple. Most people struggle to see that, just like in a game of Red-Light, Green-Light, to control your own life you must prove yourself to the people who are authority figures in your life.

When people have in-charge positions, they're called *authority figures*. By earning an in-charge position, and doing that job correctly, they become *righteous authority*. Because the winner of a Red-Light, Green-Light contest has followed rules and performed at a high level, they're given the in-charge position. Yelling out "red-light" or "green-light" is a power almost everyone has. If they're not the in-charge person, they have no authority and shouldn't be listened to. Even if they're standing at the finish line doing exactly what the in-charge person should be doing, they wouldn't be righteous authority because the job wasn't earned the right way. This is how the world works.

When you're a kid, it's normal for adults to have control over what power you use. Because of this, teachers feel authorized to use their power in ways that aren't right. I'm not talking about them doing bad things. What I mean is that they're in-charge as your teacher, they can't just make you do whatever they want. When teachers work to control things that aren't rightfully theirs to control, they're using power in areas where they don't have authority.

WHAT AUTHORITY DO TEACHERS HAVE?

Teachers have the authority to control things that can impact

> **Teachers don't have control over you like you're their property.**

the environment where students get an education. If something can change how educational an experience is, teachers have the authority to do something about it. By doing this, they're working to keep experiences productive so you can get a high-quality education. When a teacher tries to control something that isn't disrupting how educational an experience is, they're trying to control more than their in-charge position allows them to. Teachers don't have control over you like you're their property. They have permission to be an authority figure when they focus on educational goals and keeping the school safe.

A teacher can't predict what a second grader might do because, often, a second grader doesn't even know. It makes sense for rules to be stricter in younger classes because kids can get hurt if they're not. Following rules and being obedient are necessary for safety. However, don't let obedience, rule following, and staying out of trouble program you to let other people think for you. As you get older and embrace becoming a student, you should be learning to control your own educational pursuit. No one is more responsible for your education than you are, but you can't do that until you have authority to use your power.

WHAT AUTHORITY DO I HAVE TO USE MY POWER?

The authority you prove you can handle having will determine what power you can use. I've told you before, not controlling your life gives someone else the authority to do it. Don't drive your car correctly, the court can take your license.

Can't solve a disagreement without starting a fight, the police have no problem locking you up. When you're young, people do things for you out of habit. Parents don't sit around thinking about how to run their kids' lives because it's fun. They end up doing it when kids haven't shown they can do so without issues often enough. Until righteous authority figures trust you to control your own life, they'll control it for you to keep everybody safe.

Self-discipline determines how much authority you'll be given by authority figures. When you become a *student*, self-discipline determines how much control you have in getting your education. Self-discipline is what makes getting an education possible. It

> **Self-discipline is what makes getting an education possible.**

also gives you permission to demand better from this broken system. To make sure you're being self-disciplined in your decision-making, ask yourself these questions:

SELF-DISCIPLINE ASSESSMENT
1) Do I have the power to do this?
2) Do I know how to do this correctly without issues?
3) Do I know if a righteous authority figure would support me doing this?

WHAT HAPPENS WHEN I'M SELF-DISCIPLINED?

When you have self-discipline, you become a righteous authority figure in your own life. This proves to the adults in your life that you're ready to start taking responsibility for your own life. So, when you're at school, this makes your thoughts on what goes on in the classroom just as important as any teacher. If you feel like education is missing from your experience, you don't need to wait on other people to make things right. If your teachers don't include education in their plans, they stop being righteous authority figures. The system says education is their goal, but it hasn't made education the focus of how things operate. I give you permission to fight against this kind of experience. Saying education is the goal while focusing on *Institutionalized Academic Obedience* is a lack of integrity. If this broken system is ever going to change, their hypocrisy needs to be confronted.

CHAPTER SIX:
DON'T ACCEPT NO

ARE TEACHERS HYPOCRITES?

The brokenness of the system sets teachers up to be hypocrites. The word education is written all over most schools' mission statements, vision statements, and webpages. The highest authority figures in the profession say getting an education is the most important thing a kid can do. For this reason, a lack of educational integrity goes against everything the system says it wants. As a student, the authority figure you deal with most is the teacher. Hypocrisy is everywhere in this broken system, but it gets passed down until teachers are stuck looking like the ones who lack integrity.

> **The brokenness of the system sets teachers up to be hypocrites.**

Understand, the teacher may not actually be the hypocrite. It's fairer to say they're the people who you deal with most in a system of hypocrisy. Remember, teachers don't get trained or licensed to educate. They are certified caregivers, instructors, evaluators, and classroom managers. Because the system talks so much about how important education is, it's hard to accept that teachers work so hard in this profession without being clear on what education really is. That's what teachers are most guilty of.

No one says, "We want to teach a lot of lessons and give kids a bunch of information they'll probably never use." The system says it wants kids to get an education so they can live successful lives. Society says it wants kids to be prepared for adulthood. If this is true, how can we call it anything but hypocrisy when a teacher's actions make getting an education harder to do. Since I'm giving you bad news, I need to be clear. I don't want to be disrespectful to teachers or the teaching profession. I really mean that. However, someone needs to be held responsible when school becomes a hard place to get an education.

WHY BLAME TEACHERS IF THE SYSTEM IS BROKEN?

Teachers are not to blame for the brokenness of the system, but no one else is with student's often enough in school to change their experience. Teachers decide how things go in the classroom. Their ideas control how your days go. When teachers tell students their expectations for the year, those plans also suggest what higher authority figures want. As a baby boss in the education system, a teacher's plans need to be in line with what big bosses want. When education is the focus of what big bosses talk about, but not what baby bosses are qualified to do, the system's hypocrisy lands in the teacher's lap.

The longer you go to school, the more you'll want to ask questions like, "Why am I learning this," or, "When will I ever use this?" When teacher's give you problems to solve, projects to complete, and essays to write, it can be a lot. "History is so boring – I hate it," is the only way a lot of kids know how to say, "If I knew the educational value of a lesson on Ancient Egypt, I might just appreciate learning about it." When teachers don't tell students the uses and benefits of the information being taught, they hide the education students are trying to get. A student who sees this hypocrisy is right to ask questions. Raise your hand and ask these questions if you can't see how to use or benefit from the information a teacher is teaching:

EDUCATIONAL VALUE CHECK
1) How do I connect this information to my actual life?
2) How do I use this information in the real-world?
3) How do I benefit from learning this in the real-world?

For you to attend school, follow instructions, complete your work, and not know how to use or benefit from what you're learning is wrong. If this is your regular experience in K-12 schools, you'll be graduating with less than 50% of an education. You deserve better. If this is your experience, a demand needs to be made. Asking these questions will help you decide if you have a good reason to make one:

SHOULD I MAKE A DEMAND
1) Have I been a student?
2) Have I been looking for *Educational Value*?
3) Have I been given less than a complete education?
4) Have I tried to get help and fix the problem?

HOW DO I MAKE A DEMAND?
You make a demand by letting authority figures know someone or something is making it difficult for you to get an education. This is done to put your educational pursuit back on track. You need to write down:

1) What the problem is
2) How the problem is connected to your education

3) The people responsible for fixing the problem
4) Any solution you've already tried
5) The solution you now want (include a deadline)

A demand is not whining to your friends or pouting on social media. It's not crying to your parents, "Please get me out of that class – I don't like that teacher!" It's an official complaint made to righteous authority to correct issues that are making education difficult to get.

Humanity's biggest moments have happened when people wanted to change something that limited or upset them. The way they complained helped determine how problems got solved. Refusing to support a student with the right space or opportunities is very wrong, but letting anger and disrespect fuel your actions will probably get you in trouble. If getting a better education is really what you want, talk to the person who's making things difficult for you and try to find a solution. If that doesn't work, find their boss and tell them your issue. Keep talking to higher authority figures until someone helps you fix the problem. Trying to get revenge is not the point. Seeing someone lose their job is not your goal. You're a student who wants an education; correct? Then you should make a demand like this:

> **A demand is not whining to your friends or pouting on social media.**

EDUCATION COMPLAINT
Problem:
My math class is loud and too much playing is going on.
Connection To Education:
Classroom rules say worktime is voice level 0 or 1.

Don't Accept No

Chapter Six

Person Responsible:
My teacher – Ms. Hansen.

Solution You Tried:
I asked her to get the class quiet. My mom emailed her. I ask students to be quiet, but they don't listen.

Solution You Want:
I need a class without these distractions and a teacher who can manage the classroom by next quarter.

WHAT HAPPENS AFTER I MAKE A DEMAND?

When you make a demand, it can be approved, refused, or ignored. Righteous authority figures will work with you and try their best to get you what you're asking for. If they're willing to work with you, they are agreeing that there's an issue that needs some attention. If they decide to give you exactly what you demand, thank them and be done with the issue. If an authority figure tries to refuse or ignore your request, then you have more of a fight on your hands. For this fight, you want to make sure you have the support of others. When you make a demand for your education, you are asking for something that

> ...thank them and be done with the issue.

has already been promised to you. If an authority figure refuses or ignores you, they are allowing something else to be more important than education. Fighting for your education is something your allies will be happy to do if this ever happens.

Don't Accept No

CHAPTER SEVEN:
CALL FOR BACKUP

WHO ARE MY ALLIES?

Any person or group that agrees to help you accomplish a goal is an ally. Not just random people helping you sometimes in unplanned ways, but a partnership based on an agreement. These specific people, who agree to be there for you in specific ways, will help you make it through life successfully. The only thing you can accomplish in life on your own is failure. For everything else, you will need the help of others. Letting other people help you is a smart, mature decision. When you don't have power, authority, or a certain resource, asking for help is the way to continue progressing. The only way to avoid failure when you are in need is by using an ally's influence (their power, authority, or resources).

> **The only thing you can accomplish in life on your own is failure.**

Being in need puts you in a position of weakness, but it doesn't mean you are weak. Because of your position, you need allies to protect and uplift you. It's like football. The quarterback isn't weak, but they have five people blocking for them almost every play because their position is so unsafe. Without allies to block for them and help keep them safe, no one would ever want to be quarterback. When allies use their influence to keep you out of a position of weakness, they're holding up their end of the agreement. You hold up your end of the agreement, and show allies you can be trusted, by having student integrity. Not everyone who cares about you will be a strong ally, so you'll want to find the right people. You can ask these questions to see how strong a potential ally might be:

ALLY STRENGTH ASSESSMENT

1) Do I know them to be trustworthy and dependable?
2) Do I know why they want me to succeed?
3) Do I know what power, authority, or resource they can lend?
4) Do I know that we can speak honestly and regularly?
5) Do I know how their support could help me succeed?

HOW DO I MAKE AN ALLIANCE STRONG?

To make an alliance strong you'll need a clear agreement, loyal allies, and honest communication. As often as you can, talk with your allies to update them on your progress. Parents, family members, and friends are always asking about how school's going, what your grades are, or what you're learning. They do that for a reason. You can't look at these questions like they're meaningless chitchat or attempts to be nosey. When allies ask these questions, they're trying to strengthen the alliance. It's like them saying, "Are we still on track to reach that goal?"

You weaken your alliance by replying with incomplete answers that have no details or evidence. That's like saying, "I might not be as serious as I told you I was about that goal." This tells your ally, "I really don't need your help after all." Don't do that. Having an ally is like having a lawyer. Telling an ally that you don't really need them is like telling your lawyer you're going to court without them. That's just not smart. If you're not holding up your end of the agreement and being honest, your ally may choose to limit their influence or end the alliance. Let them know that they're needed. Let them know they're valued. Let them know, for your success, you need them to be there for you.

HOW WILL MY ALLIES BE THERE FOR ME?

In a strong alliance, your ally doesn't have to physically be there to help. If you're in a position of weakness, the influence of an ally is automatic. When your ally agrees to support you, and you hold up your end of the agreement, the two of you are like the same person in your moment of need. If I agree to help you buy groceries, I can give you my bank card, PIN number, and let you go to the store by yourself. When an ally partners with you, they are giving you permission to use their influence as your own. This is what it means for them to be there for you. Their influence becomes whatever power, authority, or resource you need at the exact moment you need it.

> **When your ally agrees to support you... the two of you are like the same person in your moment of need.**

This kind of partnership can give you unbelievable confidence because your strongest allies will be adults. Watching a kid use the influence of an adult will be weird for most adults. They won't recognize that kind of confidence coming from a kid. Because of that, they might call it disrespect. When you use an ally's influence as your own, you are no more disrespectful than that ally would be if they were there themselves. Let me give you an example:

Teacher: It's time to go back to your seat.

Student: My dad said I can call him if I have a problem.

Teacher: The issue's been dealt with already. It's time to get back to work.

Student: I'm not going to work until I call my dad.

When she was in 3rd grade, your sister told her teacher that someone pushed her in the recess line. Her teacher talked to that student, but your sister wanted to talk to me about how frustrated she was. It wouldn't be a problem for one adult to interrupt a meeting by saying, "I need to make a quick phone call to deal with an issue." That statement would probably get a response like, "Go ahead; take your time." However, since your sister was a kid, her teacher thought she could control when a phone call could be made. Your sister knew better. In an email, the teacher told me that she spoke with your sister until she was no longer frustrated. She said your sister told her that telling me about everything in an email was good enough since she was no longer upset. We talked about the situation at home that evening, and your sister was just fine.

Because we're allies, your sister was comfortable using my authority until she felt better about that issue. I'm not giving you permission to be disobedient or throw fits. Your sister didn't do those things. A request was made, and the teacher denied it. The teacher then made a request, and your sister explained why she wouldn't do it. Being rude to the teacher or just walking out of class would have been disrespectful, and neither would have been more impactful than an ally's authority. You have permission to use that same authority anytime you feel weak, unheard, or unsafe. You say, "It doesn't feel like I'm being supported. I refuse to continue until I speak to an ally." Repeat it, "It doesn't feel like I'm being supported. I refuse to continue until I speak to an ally." If you know the strength of your ally, and that you've held up your end of an alliance, never accept a "No" when you're making a demand.

> "It doesn't feel like I'm being supported. I refuse to continue until I speak to an ally."

I NEVER ACCEPT NO?

Someone trying to tell you "No", when you know you're asking for something you should be getting, is illegal. It's not really a crime, but that's how you need to look at it. "No" is not an acceptable answer if you can say:

NEVER ACCEPT NO

1) I have the integrity of a student.
2) I asked for something that will improve my education.
3) I have allies that will support this decision.

When you can say these statements honestly, you can make a demand as righteous authority in your own life. You cannot be told "No". By telling you "No", authority figures are making your education less important than what it should be. If this happens, take your demand to that authority figure's boss with a complaint for the individual who tried to tell you "No". Continue this process until you can find righteous authority who will make your education the priority it should be. This isn't about getting revenge. This is about getting what you've been promised. It's the only way to fix the system.

By not demanding the education system to fix its biggest problems, society is giving schools permission to stay broken. Education is too important to let our schools run this way. Forgive them my child, but don't let them give you less than you deserve just because they're working hard. Giving you the support you need to get an education is how a teacher really shows you they care. Because you work with teachers every day as a student, most of your demands will go to them. Whether a teacher makes things hard for you accidently or on purpose, questioning their actions and position helps to protect the system. As often as they try to say "No" to an educational demand, it's your job to reject it. Putting forth this effort, with the support of your allies, is what it's going to take for you to get your education.

CONCLUSION:
YOU OWE YOURSELF

WHAT DO I OWE MYSELF?

My child, you owe it to yourself to give your best effort in setting yourself up for a life of fulfillment. I've given you all I can in this conversation, but I'm still troubled. K-12 schools are supposed to be the perfect place to get an education. However, most of the people who call themselves educators don't know how to explain education or make it the daily focus of school. School is not supposed to be free childcare. You're not there to focus on meeting people or making friends. You don't go to school to do thirteen years of meaningless work and hangout while you wait for adulthood. School is supposed to prepare you to take authority over your adult life, but most schools fail to get the job done because there aren't any real consequences for their failure. These words are important because they will help educate you on how to get an education.

When I say *I Owe You,* I'm asking you to hold me **Accountable** for helping you get an education. Your time as a kid should educate you on life and give you more than the food, clothes, and shelter that keep you alive. I will help you use childhood to prepare yourself for adulthood.

Conclusion – 61

When I say *Help the Helper*, I'm asking you to embrace the **Truth** about education, school, and teachers. How important you are to society makes the time and space you have to prepare for adulthood very valuable. Don't let this broken system waste the time you've been given to prepare.

When I say *Become a Student*, I'm asking you to put yourself in a position of **Righteousness** that can't be ignored. If you're focused on education, caregivers and teachers will have to become educators to help you. Don't let being a kid stop you from maturing and being responsible.

When I say *Be a Student*, I'm asking you to be consistent in an unstable system so you can have **Peace**. If you prepare yourself to live up to the *Student Integrity Thoughts*, your actions will prove that you are who you say you are. Don't attend school with the mindset of a child or pupil.

When I say *Maintain the Standard*, I'm asking you to have **Faith** in the truth you now know. Asking questions, checking for *Educational Value*, and tracking honest progress keeps the focus on education. Don't let this system convince you to accept the brokenness that has become normal for them.

When I say *Be in Control*, I'm telling you how to get **Salvation** from people controlling your life. The best way to get permission to use your power is to show self-discipline and use it correctly without issues. Prove to authority figures you can be trusted to make wise decisions and control your own life.

When I say *Don't Accept No*, I'm asking you to have a fighter's **Spirit** and not settle for less than what you've been promised. Because the system says education is their focus, respectfully complain when their actions don't match up. Never feel bad for demanding what's yours.

When I say *Call for Backup*, I'm asking you to stay connected to people you can **Call On** for support. You have limits, but holding up your end of an alliance means never having to feel weak, unheard, or unsafe because of them. Don't think you have to do this work alone; get help.

When I say *You Owe Yourself*, I'm challenging you to hold yourself **Accountable** for getting the education you go to school for. Stand firm with *Student Integrity* to get the most out of this broken education system. Demand more from yourself in school to get more for yourself in life.

Doing all this is what it means for you to **Demand It**. If you use them correctly, these words can be the education you need to find success in a broken system. If all the kids in K-12 schools were students, things would have to change. There would be no other way for a school to run well enough to support them. I am troubled because, as a student, you'll have more understanding on what education is than most of the people who will be teaching you. This makes you a threat. Even though no one is happy with most things that have become normal in schools, teachers might see you as difficult or annoying for challenging them. Maybe that's what it will take for the system to see what getting an education *really* means. Challenging this broken system is the best way to get what you deserve – what you are owed. Now, if you're prepared, let's see you go to school and get *your* education.

Power concedes nothing without a demand.

Frederick Douglas

ABOUT THE AUTHOR

Daniel C. Manley is an American educator, author, speaker, and educational provocateur who has made it his life's work to make the attainment of a high-quality education a real possibility for all young people. As a mentor, teacher, and administrator, he has served the middle school and high school population for nearly twenty years. As Co-Founder and CEO of Stand & Withstand Integrity Group, he has made it his mission to empower and prepare children to be firmly planted, deeply rooted, and properly positioned as adults with an education that allows for them to achieve practical success.

Also Available
WISDOM & INSTRUCTION:
Education Receipt Book

RECORD IT:
What "How Was School Today" Really Means
Educational Reflection Journal

For Booking
Stand & Withstand Integrity Group LLC
P.O. Box 782771
Wichita, KS 67278

CONTACT@STANDWITHSTAND.ORG

www.ingramcontent.com/pod-product-compliance
Lightning Source LLC
Chambersburg PA
CBHW020244010526
44107CB00002B/93